Josephine's
CATASTROPHES

Three Great Cat Tales

Published by Silver Press,
an imprint of Silver Burdett Press,
A Simon & Schuster Company
299 Jefferson Road, Parsippany, NJ 07054
Printed in the United States of America

10 9 8 7 6 5 4 3 2 1

Individual stories originally published in separate
editions as follows:

Josephine's Night Out,
text © 1991 Silver, Burdett & Ginn Inc.
art © 1991 Daniel Vasconcellos

Josephine Takes A Spin,
text © 1992 Silver, Burdett & Ginn Inc.
first edition art © 1992 Daniel Vasconcellos

Josephine Finds A Friend,
text © 1992 Silver, Burdett & Ginn Inc.
art © 1992 Daniel Vasconcellos

Library of Congress Cataloging-in-Publication Data
Marion, D.
    Josephine's Catastrophes: Three Great Cat Tales/D.
Marion; illustrated by Daniel Vasconcellos.
p. cm.
    Contents: Josephine's Night Out—Josephine Takes
A Spin—Josephine Finds A Friend.
    Summary: Josephine the mischievous cat causes
her young owner to worry and fret in these three
rhyming stories.
    1. Children's stories, American. [1. Cats—Fiction.
2. Stories in rhyme.] I. Vasconcellos, Daniel, ill.
II. Title
PZ8.3.M39143Jo   1995
[E]—dc20   94-30493   CIP   AC
ISBN 0-382-24908-9 (LSB)   ISBN 0-382-24909-7 (JHC)
ISBN 0-382-24910-0 (S/C)

Josephine's CATASTROPHES

Three Great Cat Tales

stories by D. Marion

illustrations by Daniel Vasconcellos

Silver Press
Parsippany, New Jersey

Josephine's Night Out

There is no doubt about

who let the little cat get out.

The wind was blowing,
the snow was snowing,

but my Josephine just kept on going.

"Josephine, come back," I said.

"It's warm in here.
It's time for bed."

Fred and I sat down to wait
till Mother came and said, "It's late."

Then Dad came in to say, "Goodnight.
Josephine will be all right."

I could not sleep, for in my head

I thought of Josephine,
cold and dead.

Soon the night turned into day.
The wind and snow had gone away.

I looked around and there I found . . .

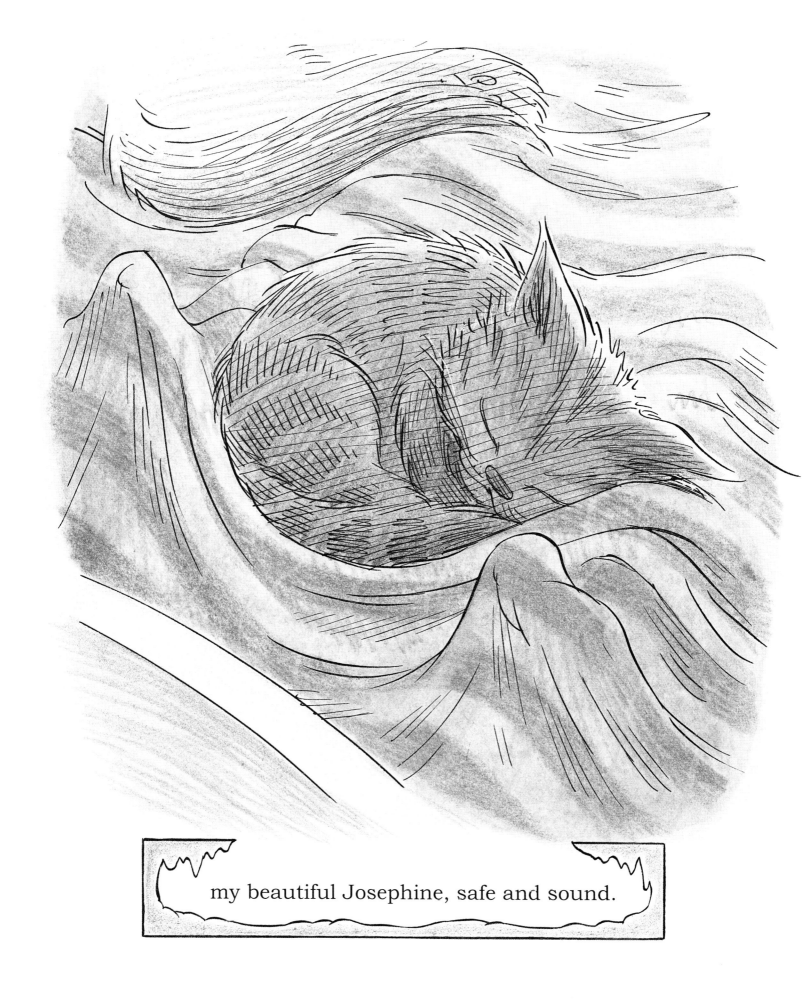

my beautiful Josephine, safe and sound.

Josephine Takes a Spin

There is not a doubt at all

who chased Josephine down the hall.

Down into the cellar she flew,
and where she went no one knew.

"Josephine, you're wet," I cried.

"That's no reason for you to hide."

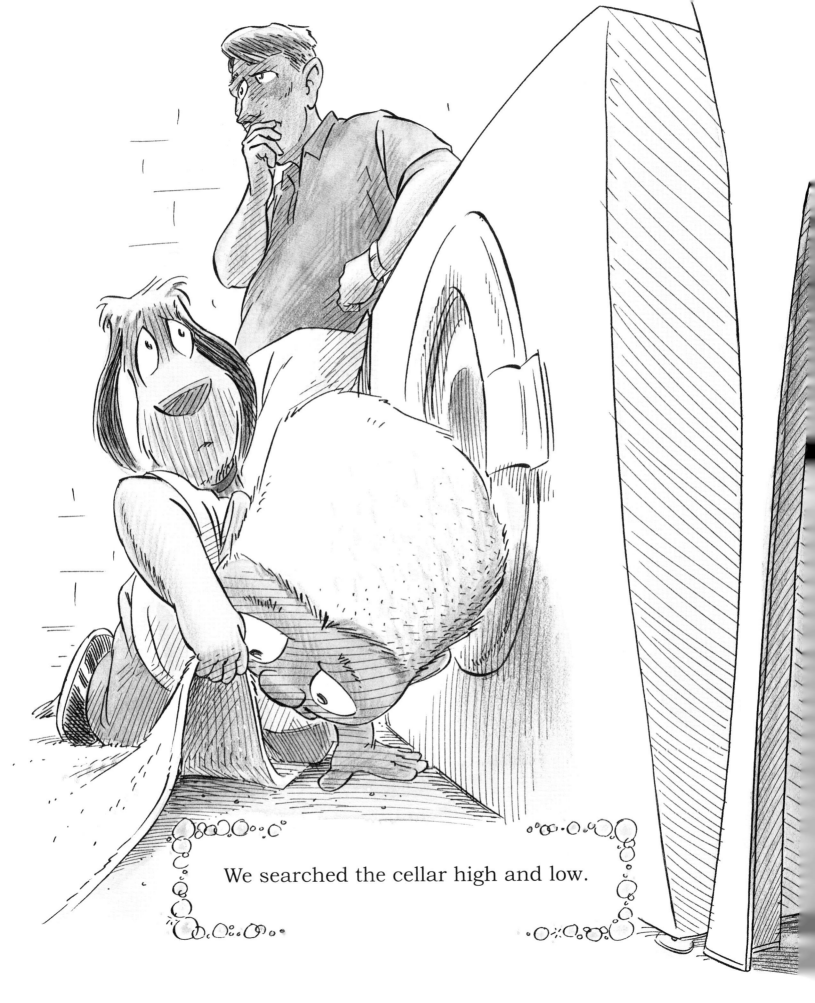

We searched the cellar high and low.

But that silly cat just wouldn't show.

Dad said, "Let's go and watch TV. Josephine will show up, you'll see."

We all sat down to watch the show,
when suddenly Dad cried out, "Oh no!"

"The dryer! One place we didn't look.
If she's there, she'll really cook!"

I could not speak, for in my head

I thought of Josephine, dry but dead.

Dad ran fast, but I ran faster.
And in our hurry, we almost passed her.

I looked around, and way up high,

was my beautiful Josephine,
safe and dry.

Josephine
Finds a Friend

There is no doubt who broke the rule
and let the cat get out at school.

Down she went, and in and out.
I tried to stop Josephine with a shout.

Up in the lunchroom it was very loud.
Josephine hissed when she saw the crowd.
Then she stopped and found a treat.

She went to the nurse and rubbed his feet.

She jumped from the closet shelf to the floor.
Then she ran through the principal's door.

I ran as fast as I could go,
but I was stopped by Mrs. Low.
She said, "You can't see Mr. Malone.
He's busy now. He's on the phone."

PRINCIPAL
Mr. Malone
←

"My cat's in there," I blurted out.
"I know," she said. "I saw her there.
She jumped right up on the principal's chair."

I could not answer, for in my head
I thought of Josephine, squashed and dead.

At last we went in, and I wanted to clap.
My beautiful Josephine...

was taking a nap.